Holiday and Seasonal Crafts from Recycled Materials

from the Choose to Reuse Series

Written by Deborah Whitacre and Becky Radtke

Illustrated by Becky Radtke

Teaching & Learning Company

1204 Buchanan St., P.O. Box 10
Carthage, IL 62321

This book belongs to

_____

This book is dedicated to my children Mindy, Amanda and Ryan—Deborah

This is for my children Michelle and Angela—Becky

We would like to thank Bubs Kennedy, our teacher consultant,
for the valuable contributions she made to this book.

This book was developed for the Teaching & Learning Company
by The Good Neighbor Press, Inc., Grand Junction, CO.

Cover photo by Images and More Photography

Copyright © 1995, Teaching & Learning Company

ISBN No. 1-57310-027-7

Printing No. 98765432

**Teaching & Learning Company
1204 Buchanan St., P.O. Box 10
Carthage, IL 62321**

Table of Contents

The crafts pictured on the front cover are the Breezy Butterfly (page 36), the Sensational Scarecrow Centerpiece (page 10) and the Spectacular Snow Globe (page 30).

Dear Teacher or Parent,

Recycling is on everyone's minds these days. We are all trying hard to pull together to protect and preserve the Earth for future generations. This book offers you the unique opportunity to involve your students in this effort. It is our hope that your students will discover how they, too, can be an important part of saving their planet. What better way to show them the benefits of choosing to reuse than by creating these fun craft projects?

The crafts in this book all use items that the average household often throws away. (You'll notice that throughout this book an asterisk has been placed by each item that is being recycled.) The easy-to-follow instructions will help you to guide your students in turning recyclable items into super seasonal crafts. Each craft comes illustrated and (if necessary) with reproducible patterns. For safety reasons, we advise you to closely supervise your students while they make the crafts in this book. Use your good judgement and consider the child's age and ability to modify certain steps or processes when you feel it is necessary. Always carefully read and follow the directions and warnings given on the labels of materials you use. All of these crafts can be used to help children learn about the different seasons of the year.

At the back of this book you will find a fun, reproducible certificate. For your convenience, we have also included reproducible letters to parents and guardians requesting that they please send or stop sending household recyclable items.

As the owner of this book, you are entitled and welcomed to use all the art contained for classroom purposes (wall and door decorations, bulletin board designs, flyers, invitations, etc.). We hope that this book will be used and enjoyed by you over and over again during your teaching career.

Sincerely,

Becky & Deborah

Deborah Whitacre
Becky Radtke

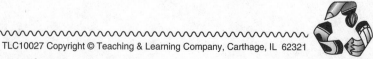

Breakfast for Birds

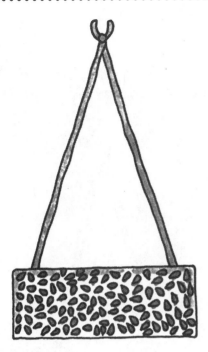

■ Perfect Timing

Make this craft when studying fall, animals or when reading:

- *Feathers for Lunch.* Lois Ehlert. Harcourt Brace Jovanovich, 1990.
- *Flap Your Wings and Try.* Charlotte Pomerantz. Lippincott, 1989.
- *Antler, Bear, Canoe: A Northwood Alphabet Year.* Betsy Bowen. Little, Brown. Joy Street Books, 1991.

■ Materials Needed

- toilet paper tube*
- peanut butter
- birdseed
- newspapers
- piece of yarn
- scissors

■ Tell the Class

"In fall, squirrels gather food and store it for the winter ahead. Many birds will fly south where it will be warm. But some birds stay behind. When the ground is covered with snow, it isn't as easy for them to find things to eat.

I'll show you how to make a treat for the birds. You can take it home and have an adult hang it from a tree branch."

■ How to Make It

For Teachers, Aides and Parent Volunteers

A. Cut a ½" (1.27 cm) slit into both ends of a tissue tube. Prepare a tube like this for each student.

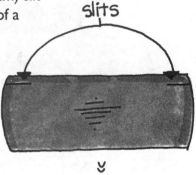

B. Spread newspapers on the floor and pour small piles of birdseed on them.

C. Cut 23" (58.42 cm) pieces of yarn. Every student will need one piece.

■ How to Make It

For Students

1. Spread peanut butter all over the toilet tissue tube.

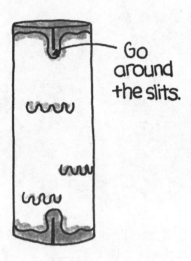

2. Roll the tube in a pile of birdseed until it is completely covered. Let it dry completely.

3. Put the yarn through the tube and knot the ends together. Secure the yarn into each slit (so it won't move around) as shown. (Younger students will need assistance.)

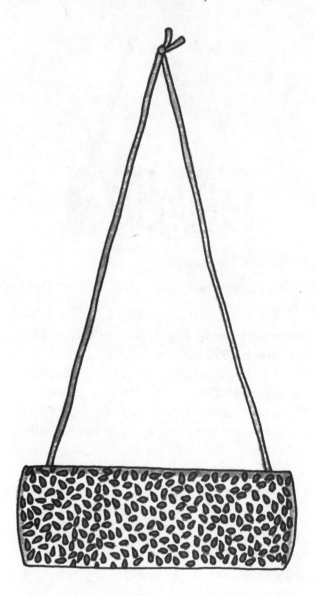

4. Have your mom or dad hang it on a tree branch for the birds. When all the seed is eaten off, apply a fresh coat of peanut butter and roll it in birdseed again.

Gang of Ghosts Garland

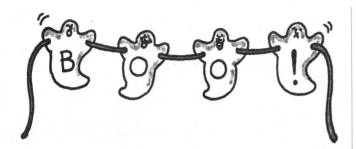

■ Perfect Timing

Make this craft when studying fall, Halloween or when reading:

- *Ghost in a Four-Room Apartment.* Ellen Raskin. Atheneum Publishers, 1969.
- *A Ghost Named Fred.* Nathaniel Benchley. Harper & Row, 1968.
- *A Circle of Seasons.* Ann Nolan Clark. Farrar, Straus, Giroux, 1970.

■ Materials Needed

- 2 sheets of bacon plastic* (the thin pieces that come inside packages of bacon)
- paper punch
- black piece of yarn
- orange washable marker
- black, fine-tipped washable marker
- tape
- reproducible ghost patterns (page 5)
- scissors

■ Tell the Class

"Many of us enjoy listening to spooky stories at Halloween. Sometimes the stories are about haunted houses and ghosts.

Would you like to make a string of ghosts? When you're done, you can take it home to use as a Halloween decoration."

■ How to Make It

For Teachers, Aides and Parent Volunteers

A. Photocopy the ghost patterns (page 5) for each student. 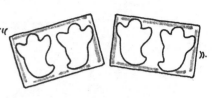 Cut on the dotted line to make two halves. Each student will need one half.

B. Cut 31" (78.74 cm) pieces of black yarn. Every student will need one piece.

■ How to Make It

For Students

1. Cut out the paper ghost patterns. Use the black marker to trace the pattern onto the bacon plastic sheets. Trace four ghosts and cut them out. (You can fit two ghosts on one bacon plastic sheet.)

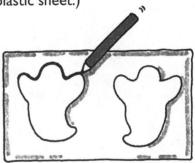

2. Stack all the ghosts and paper-punch a hole in each arm as shown.

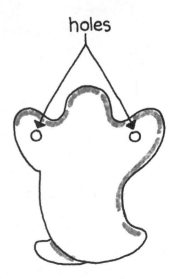

holes

3. Use the black marker to draw a different expression on each ghost.

Examples

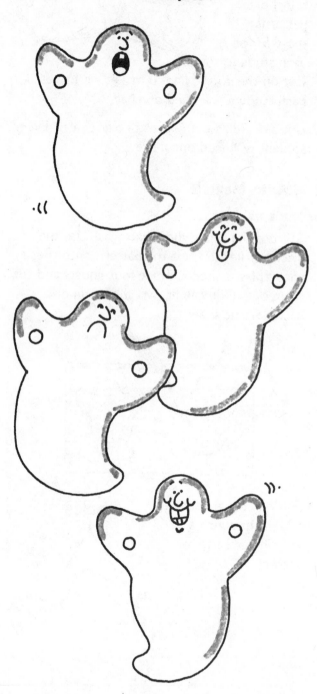

4. Thread the black yarn through the holes. Space the ghosts evenly apart and secure them with a piece of tape on the back.

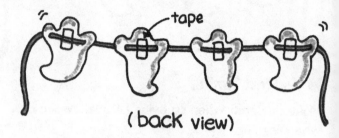

(back view)

5. Use the orange marker to write *Boo!* on the ghosts as shown.

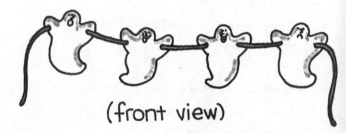

(front view)

6. Take your ghost garland home and hang it across a window or door as a Halloween decoration.

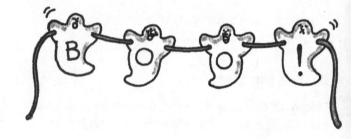

Ghost Patterns

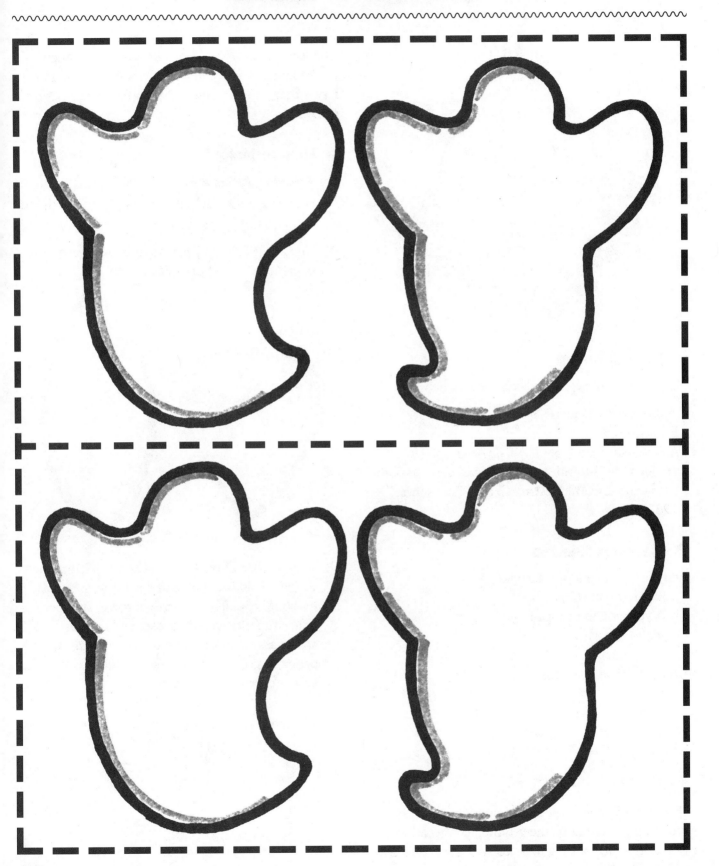

TLC10027 Copyright © Teaching & Learning Company, Carthage, IL 62321

Nifty Nature Necklace

■ Perfect Timing

Make this craft when studying fall or when reading:

- *Nature Walk.* Douglas Florian. Greenwillow Books, 1989.
- *A Busy Year.* Leo Lionni. Alfred A. Knopf, 1992.
- *Through the Year with Harriet: A Time Concept Book.* Betsy and Giulio Maestro. Crown Publishers, 1985.

■ Materials Needed

- lunch bag* (used but unsoiled)
- 3 paper towel stampers
- red, yellow and orange tempera paint
- piece of brown yarn
- paper punch
- reproducible leaf patterns
- pencil
- newspapers
- shallow bowls
- scissors

■ Tell the Class

"Fall is a wonderful time of year. Leaves turn beautiful colors and sail to the ground. The weather gets cooler so that we need to wear sweaters or jackets. And did you notice that it gets dark earlier?

Let's create some fall leaves of our own. When you're finished, you can punch holes in them and string them onto a piece of yarn to make a nature necklace."

■ How to Make It

For Teachers, Aides and Parent Volunteers

A. Photocopy the leaf patterns below for each student.

B. Cut 26" (66.04 cm) pieces of brown yarn. Each student will need one piece.

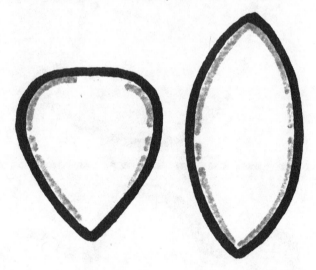

C. Take a piece of paper towel and roll it up as shown. Fold it in half and cinch the middle with masking tape. This is a paper towel stamper. Your students will dip these into tempera paint and press them down onto their lunch bag paper to create interesting splotches. Every student will need three stampers.

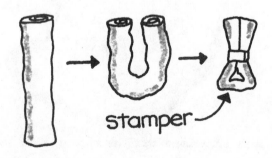

stamper

D. Spread newspapers on all surfaces where students will be working. Fill shallow bowls with red, yellow and orange tempera paint that students can share. Three students can share three bowls. Place the bowls on newspaper.

■ How to Make It

For Students

1. Open the lunch bag so that it sits flat. Choose a corner seam and cut it from top to bottom. Continue cutting all the way around the bottom of the bag. Discard the bottom. You should end up with one flat piece of brown paper. (Younger students will need assistance.)

2. Take one of your paper towel stampers and dip it (just a little) into the bowl of red tempera paint. Hold the stamper above the bowl to let the excess paint drip off. Then press the stamper down all over the brown paper. When you are finished, repeat this step with the yellow and orange paint. Use a clean stamper for each color.
When you have covered the brown paper with paint, let it dry.

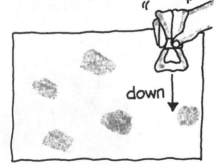

3. Cut out the leaf patterns. Use a pencil to trace around them onto the brown paper. Cut the leaves out and paper-punch a hole in each.

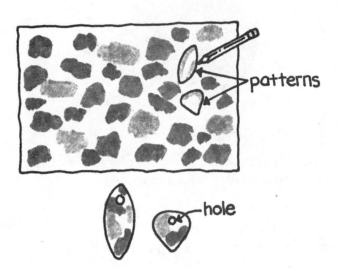

4. String the leaves onto the piece of yarn. Knot the ends together to make a necklace. (Younger students will need assistance.)

5. Wear your nature necklace at home. See if family members can guess how you made it!

Personal Apple

■ Perfect Timing

Make this craft at the beginning of the school year, when studying fall, Halloween or when reading:

- *The Seasons of Arnold's Apple Tree*. Gail Gibbons. Harcourt Brace Jovanovich, 1984.
- *A Book of Seasons*. Alice and Martin Provensen. Random House, 1982.
- *Apple Picking Time*. Michelle Benoit Slawson. Crown, 1994.

■ Materials Needed

- frozen juice lid* (12 oz. [354.9 ml]), metal
- cereal box* (Eighteen students can share one.)
- square of red construction paper
- strip of green construction paper
- piece of brown pipe cleaner
- pencil
- black crayon or washable fine-tipped black marker
- masking tape
- tape
- scissors

■ Tell the Class

"I can tell just by looking at everyone, that I have a wonderful bunch of students. We're going to do a lot of learning this school year!

I have some learning to do myself. I need to learn your names. You can help me by making an apple craft today. When you are finished, I'll tape it onto your table spot (or desk). These apples will help you, too. You'll always know where to sit."

■ How to Make It

For Teachers, Aides and Parent Volunteers

A. Cut 3½" x 3½" (8.89 x 8.89 cm) squares of red construction paper. Every student will need one square.

B. Cut 4" x 1½" (10.16 x 3.81 cm) strips of cardboard from cereal boxes. Each student will need one strip.

C. Cut 1" x ¾" (2.54 x 1.91 cm) strips of green construction paper. Each student will need one strip.

■ How to Make It

For Students

1. Use a pencil to trace around the juice lid onto the square of red construction paper. Cut it out. This is the apple.

2. Use a black crayon or washable fine-tipped marker to write your first name and the first letter of your last name onto the apple.

3. Make four masking tape loops and put them onto the back of the apple. Press it firmly down onto the juice lid.

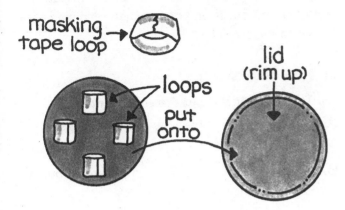

masking tape loop

loops put onto

lid (rim up)

4. Fold the green construction paper strip in half. Cut off the corners as shown. Unfold it. These are the leaves. (Younger students will need assistance.)

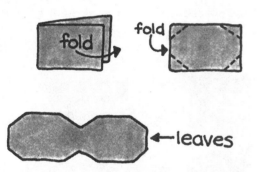

fold

fold

leaves

5. Use a bit of tape to attach the leaves to the piece of pipe cleaner (the stem). Masking tape the stem to the juice lid (the back of the apple) as shown.

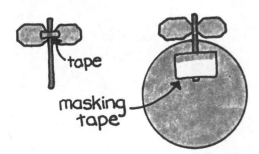

tape

masking tape

6. Fold the strip of cardboard in half. Use masking tape to attach it to the juice lid as shown. This will make the apple stand up. (Younger students will need assistance.)

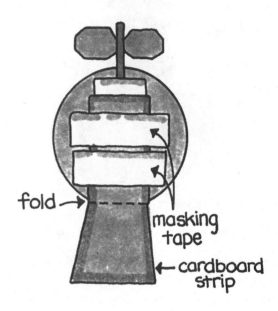

fold

masking tape

cardboard strip

7. Wait for your teacher to come and tape your apple to your table spot (or desk). Use the apples to learn classmates' names. Later, when your teacher no longer needs to look at the apple to know your name, you can take it home as a keepsake.

David J.

masking tape

Sensational Scarecrow Centerpiece

■ Perfect Timing

Make this craft when studying fall or reading:

• *Jeb Scarecrow's Pumpkin Patch.* Jana Dillon. Houghton Mifflin, 1992.
• *The Scarebird.* Sid Fleischman. Greenwillow Books, 1983.
• *Autumn.* Lois Santrey. Troll Associates, 1983.

Materials Needed

• 1 craft stick*
• 2 small, flat buttons
• 1 small lump of clay
• reproducible scarecrow patterns (page 12)
• peanut butter jar lid* (1lb. 2 oz. [504 g])
• strip of burlap
• scraps of white felt
• scraps of yellow yarn
• crayons or washable markers
• glue
• scissors

■ Tell the Class

"Did you know that a long time ago farmers used to hire people to stand in their fields, clap their hands and scare away birds? Many farmers couldn't afford to hire someone, so they made pretend "people" called scarecrows instead.

Today you will get to make a scarecrow of your own. You can put it on your kitchen or dining room table as a centerpiece."

■ How to Make It

For Teachers, Aides and Parent Volunteers

A. Photocopy the scarecrow patterns (page 12) for every student.

B. Cut ⅝" x 3¾" (1.59 x 9.53 cm) strips of burlap. Each student will need one strip.

■ How to Make It

For Students

1. Color the scarecrow and felt strip pattern and cut them out. Glue the burlap strip to the back of the scarecrow's arms as shown. Use scissors to "fringe" edges that hang out.

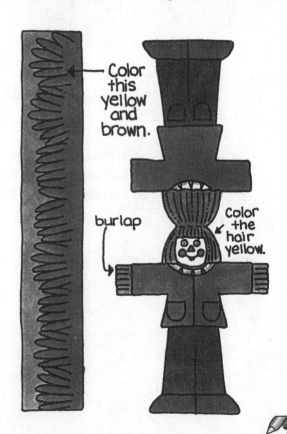

Color this yellow and brown.

burlap

Color the hair yellow.

2. Glue the scarecrow pattern together as shown.

Glue in between and press together.

3. Glue scraps of yellow yarn onto the hair areas.

(front)   (back)

4. Cut small squares of felt and glue them onto the scarecrow's pants as patches. (Younger students can skip this step.) Glue the buttons onto the collar.

5. Tape the craft stick to the back of the scarecrow. Leave about 1" (2.54 cm) of the stick showing at the bottom.

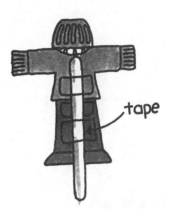

tape

6. Press the lump of clay down onto the center of the peanut butter jar lid.

clay

7. Push the craft stick into the clay to make the scarecrow stand. Put the felt strips inside the lid and tape the seam together.

8. Take your scarecrow home and use it as an eye-catching centerpiece.

Scarecrow Patterns

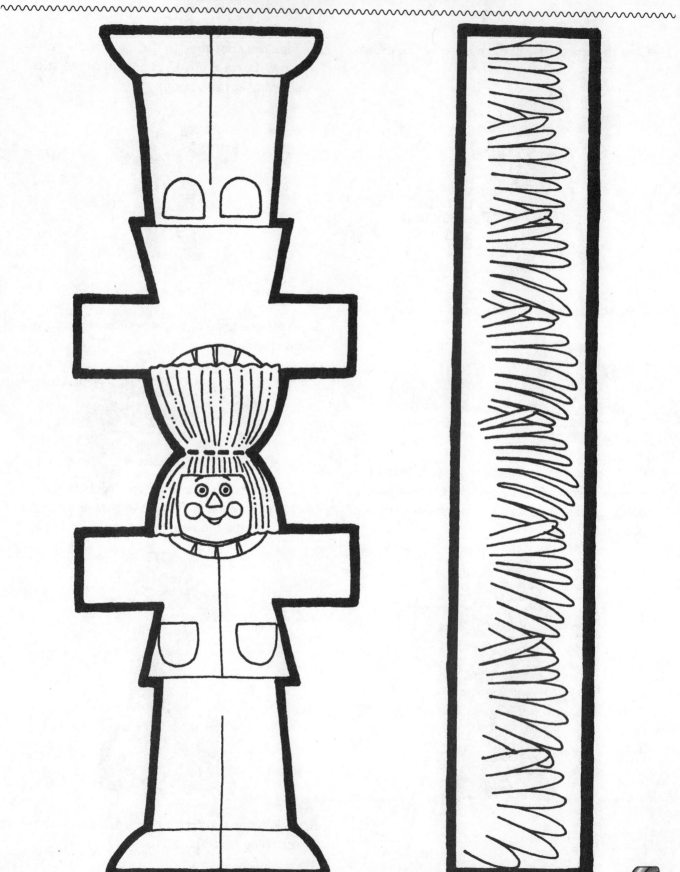

Smart Smock

■ Perfect Timing

Make this craft at the beginning of the school year or when reading:

• *Sunshine Makes the Seasons.* Franklyn M. Branley. T.Y. Crowell, 1974.
• *The Day the Teacher Went Bananas.* James Howe. Dutton, 1984.
• *Thirteen Moons on a Turtle's Back.* Joseph Bruchac. Philomel, 1992.

■ Materials Needed

• white or light colored button-up shirt*
• various colors of fabric paint bottles—the kind that you can squeeze and write with. (To help with the cost, you may want to ask for a small amount of money from each child.)
• newspapers

■ Tell the Class

"Welcome to my class! We are going to be doing lots of interesting art projects this year! They will be fun but sometimes messy.

For your very first art project you will be making a shirt that you can wear so that you can keep your clothes clean. Start thinking about what you'd like to draw on your shirt!"

■ How to Make It

For Teachers, Aides and Parent Volunteers

A. Carefully read the directions given on the fabric paint bottles. They should tell you how to use them, how long the paint needs to dry, any health hazards, etc. They may also give directions on how to pre-wash the fabric (in this case a shirt), before applying the paint. (Send a note home to parents with this information. This way students will bring shirts that are ready to have fabric paints applied to them. You may also want to request that parents iron the shirts before sending them. It's easier for the children to write and draw on pressed fabric.)

B. Spread newspapers to protect desk or table surfaces where students will be working.

C. Go to a secondhand store and get shirts that students can wear while making their Smart Smocks.

D. Make a Smart Smock for yourself! Have all your students sign it and be sure to include the date. It will be useful and serve as a memento of your class at the end of the year.

■ How to Make It

For Students

1. Use a fabric paint bottle to print your first name and first letter of your last name on the front of your shirt. (Younger students will need assistance.)

Like this

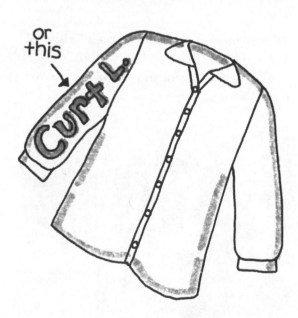

or this

2. Use your imagination and the various colored fabric paint bottles to draw things (such as an ice-cream cone, rocket, balloon, etc.), shapes and designs onto the front of your shirt. Your teacher will tell you how long the paint will need to dry. (He or she may want you to decorate the back of your shirt another day.)

idea for the back

Tuna Can Turkey

◼ Perfect Timing

Make this craft when studying fall, Thanksgiving or when reading:

- *One Tough Turkey: A Thanksgiving Story.* Steven Kroll. Holiday House, 1984.
- *A Turkey for Thanksgiving.* Eve Bunting. Clarion Books, 1991.
- *Mousekin's Thanksgiving.* Edna Miller. Prentice-Hall, 1985.

◼ Materials Needed

- tuna can* (empty and clean)
- 3 colored craft feathers
- crayons
- 2 wiggly eyes (5 mm size)
- reproducible turkey patterns (page 17)
- strips of brown construction paper
- tape
- glue
- scissors

◼ Tell the Class

"Thanksgiving is a time for us to think about the many, many things we have in our lives to be thankful for. We can be thankful for our health, our families, our country and our school. People usually celebrate Thanksgiving with a big turkey dinner!

I'll show you how you can make a turkey centerpiece that you can put on your dinner table at Thanksgiving time."

◼ How to Make It

For Teachers, Aides and Parent Volunteers

A. Make a photocopy of the turkey patterns (page 17) for each student.

B. Cut 1½" x 11" (3.81 x 27.94 cm) strips of brown construction paper. Each student will need one strip.

◼ How to Make It

For Students

1. Color the turkey pattern pieces according to the directions given below. Cut all the pieces out.

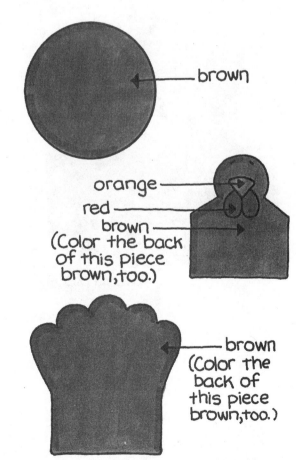

2. Turn the tuna can so it is bottom side up. Glue the brown construction paper strip around the can. Put a piece of tape on the seam to make it extra secure.

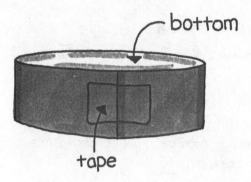

bottom

tape

3. Glue the circle pattern onto the bottom of the can. Glue the head and tail pieces on as shown.

circle

tail

head piece

4. Glue the three feathers onto the tail.

5. Glue the two wiggly eyes onto the turkey's face.

6. Take your turkey home. Use it as a centerpiece on the table at Thanksgiving.

TLC10027 Copyright © Teaching & Learning Company, Carthage, IL 62321

Turkey Patterns

Great Harmony Place Mat

■ Perfect Timing

Make this craft when studying winter, Martin Luther King, Jr., or when reading:

- *Caps, Hats, Socks and Mittens: A Book About the Four Seasons.* Louise Borden. Scholastic Inc., 1988.
- *Poems for Seasons and Celebrations.* William Cole. World Pub., 1961.
- *What Is Martin Luther King, Jr. Day?* Margot Parker. Childrens Press, Inc., 1990.

■ Materials Needed

- large brown grocery bag* (Two students can share one.)
- reproducible harmony pattern (page 20)
- magazines* (with pictures of people)
- multicultural-colored crayons
- glue
- scissors

■ Tell the Class

"Martin Luther King, Jr., was a great African American leader. He gave a very famous speech. In it he told how he dreamed of an America where people of all skin colors and beliefs would live together in harmony. *Harmony* means "in peace." He wanted everyone to be treated equally. He was admired and respected for his ideas. Every third Monday of January the United States celebrates a day in Martin Luther King, Jr.'s honor.

Let's make a place mat about living together in harmony. When you are finished you can take it home and use it at the dinner table. Tell your family about Martin Luther King, Jr. and his dream.

■ How to Make It

For Teachers, Aides and Parent Volunteers

Photocopy a harmony pattern (page 20) for every student.

■ How to Make It

For Students

1. Cut the front and back panels from the grocery bag. Give one panel to another student to use. (Younger students will need assistance.)

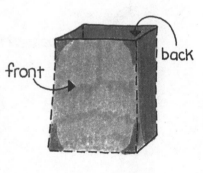
front   back

2. Place your panel horizontally (sideways). If there is a logo on it, use the other side. Use red, brown, tan, yellow, black and white crayons to color stripes on it. These colors represent different races of people. This is your place mat.

3. Color the harmony pattern. Cut it out and glue it onto the center of the place mat as shown.

4. Look through magazines. Cut out faces of people with the same and different skin colors.

5. Glue the faces all over the place mat.

6. Take your place mat home. Use it at dinner time. As you eat, think about the harmony that Martin Luther King, Jr., wanted for the world. Think about how you can help make this happen by being kind to all your classmates and playmates.

Honest Abe Canister

■ Perfect Timing

Make this craft when studying winter, Presidents' Day or when reading:

- *Abe Lincoln's Beard.* Jan Wahl. Delacorte, 1971.
- *Seasons of the Tall Grass Prairie.* Carol Lerner. Morrow, 1980.
- *Amy Loves the Snow.* Julia Hoban. Scholastic Inc., 1989.

■ Materials Needed

- juice can* (12 oz. [354.9 ml])
- black spray paint
- laundry detergent cap* (one that will fit inside the juice can)
- black and flesh-colored felt
- 2 medium sized wiggly eyes
- black fine-tipped washable marker
- red and brown washable markers
- reproducible Abraham Lincoln face patterns (page 23)
- glue
- scissors

■ Tell the Class

"America has had many different Presidents. Do you know which President has his picture on the penny? Yes, it's Abraham Lincoln.

Abraham Lincoln was so honest that some people called him "Honest Abe."

Let's make something that you can take home to put by the washing machine. It can be used to store loose change from pants and shirt pockets."

■ How to Make It

For Teachers, Aides and Parent Volunteers

(Do these steps the day before this craft is made.)

A. Spray the outside of each student's juice can and laundry detergent lid with black spray paint. Let them dry overnight.

B. Make a photocopy of the Abraham Lincoln face patterns (page 23). Cut them out and trace onto the correct felt color (see directions below). Cut them out. Each student will need a set of all felt pieces.

Cut the face and nose pieces from flesh felt.

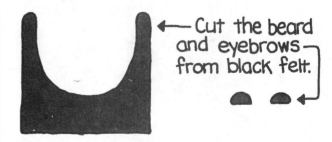

Cut the beard and eyebrows from black felt.

■ How to Make It

For Students

1. Glue the face piece onto the juice can as shown.

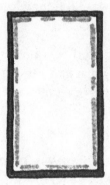

2. Glue the beard piece onto the face piece (lining up the edge with the bottom of the juice can) as shown.

3. Glue the nose and eyebrow pieces on as shown.

4. Use the red marker to draw on a smile. Use the brown marker to draw a round dot (a mole) onto the left side of the face.

5. Put the black laundry detergent cap into the juice can for his stovepipe hat. Take him home and put him in the laundry room to store loose change.

Abraham Lincoln Face Patterns

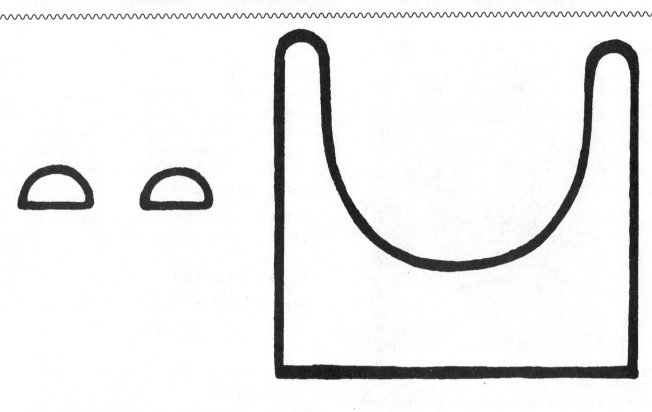

Simple Hanukkah Hanging

■ Perfect Timing

Make this craft when studying winter, Hanukkah or when reading:

- *Beni's First Chanukah.* Jane Breskin Zalben. H. Holt, 1988.
- *Grandma's Latkes.* Malka Drucker. Harcourt Brace Jovanovich, 1992.
- *Hershel and the Hanukkah Goblins.* Eric Kimmel. Holiday House, 1989.

■ Materials Needed

- large brown grocery bag* (Two students can share one.)
- menorah pattern (page 26)
- 9 halved craft sticks*
- washable markers
- tape
- glue
- scissors

■ Tell the Class

"Each winter, usually in December, Jewish families celebrate Hanukkah. During this time, they recall how, over 2,000 years ago, a small jar of oil burned in Jerusalem's temple. Even though there was only enough oil in the jar to burn for one day, it burned for eight. This amazed the Jewish army, who had recently recaptured Jerusalem. Because of this, Hanukkah lasts eight days. Each night of the celebration, Jewish families light candles which are in a stand called a menorah. There are nine candles in all—one for each day of Hanukkah and one that is used to light the others.

Today you'll make a picture of a menorah with nine pretend candles. Let's get started!"

■ How to Make It

For Teachers, Aides and Parent Volunteers

A. Photocopy a menorah pattern (page 26) for every student.

B. Snap craft sticks in half. Every student will need nine halves.

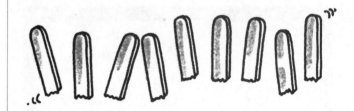

■ How to Make It

For Students

1. Cut the front and back panels from the grocery bag. Give one panel to another student to use. (Younger students will need assistance.)

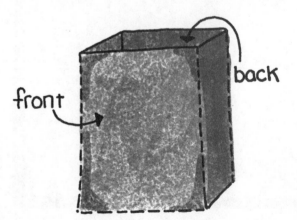

2. Color and cut out the menorah pattern on the dotted lines. Place your panel vertically (up and down), and glue the menorah onto the center as shown.

3. Use a yellow washable marker to color the rounded end portions of all the halved craft sticks. Color the remaining portions any color you wish. These are the nine candles.

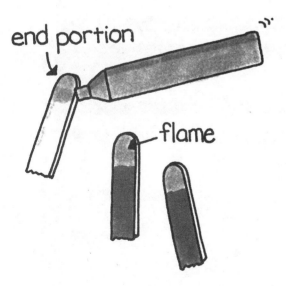

end portion

flame

4. Tape the candles onto the menorah as shown.

5. Use a washable marker to write *Happy Hanukkah* onto your picture. (Younger students will need assistance.) Take your menorah home and hang it where it can be admired.

Happy
Hanukkah

Menorah Pattern

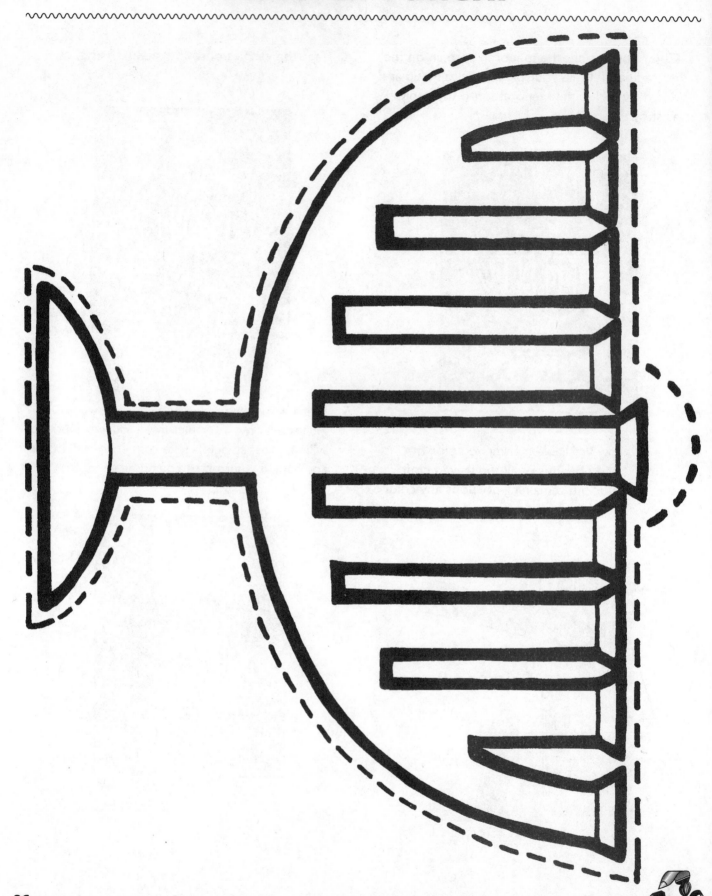

Smiling Santa Portrait

■ Perfect Timing

Make this craft when studying winter, Christmas or when reading:

• *Father Christmas.* Raymond Briggs. Coward-McCann, 1973.
• *Santa's Crash Bang Christmas.* Steven Kroll. Holiday House, 1977.
• *The Polar Express.* Chris Van Allsburg. Houghton Mifflin, 1985.

■ Materials Needed

• white Styrofoam™ tray*
• cereal box* (1 lb. 4 oz. [560 g])
  (Two students can share one.)
• reproducible Santa portrait pattern (page 29)
• paper punch
• washable markers or crayons
• glue
• scissors

■ Tell the Class

"I think everyone knows what Santa looks like! He's got a red hat that's trimmed in fur and a wonderful white moustache and beard. Santa is a very jolly fellow and always seems to be smiling!

Let's make a portrait, which is a kind of picture, of Santa. Then you can take it home and look at Santa all year long if you'd like!"

■ How to Make It

For Teachers, Aides and Parent Volunteers

A. Photocopy the Santa portrait pattern (page 29) for every student.

B. Cut a 7" x 9½" (17.78 x 24.13 cm) piece and a 1" x 9" (2.54 x 22.86 cm) piece of cardboard from a cereal box. Cut two 1" (2.54 cm) vertical slits on the bottom of each 7" x 9½" (17.78 x 24.13 cm) piece. One cereal box will make two pieces of each size. Each student will need one piece of each size.

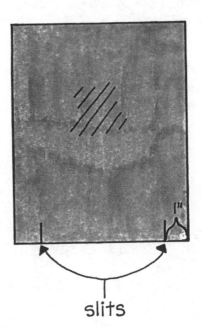

slits

■ How to Make It

For Students

1. Color (except for the hat's tassel, the hat's fur trim, the moustache and the beard) the Santa picture. Cut it out.

TLC10027 Copyright © Teaching & Learning Company, Carthage, IL 62321

2. Glue the Santa picture onto the blank side of the 7" x 9½" (17.78 x 24.13 cm) piece of cardboard (with slits at bottom).

3. Paper-punch lots of circles out of the white Styrofoam™ tray.

4. Smear glue onto Santa's hat tassel and fur trim area and also onto his moustache and beard. Place the little circles onto the glue. (Cover the areas listed completely.)

5. Draw and color green leaves and red berries around the edges of the picture.

6. Bend the 1" x 9" (2.54 x 22.86 cm) strip of cardboard in half. Insert it into the slits to make a stand. On the back, fold the ends of the stand toward each other as shown.

(front)   (back)

Santa Portrait Pattern

Spectacular Snow Globe

■ Perfect Timing

Make this craft when studying the season of winter, snow or reading:

• *The Snow Speaks.* Nancy White Carlstrom. Little, Brown, 1992.
• *Winter: Discovering the Seasons.* Lois Santrey. Troll Associates, 1983.
• *When Will It Snow?* Syd Hoff. Harper & Row, 1971.

■ Materials Needed

• small, glass baby food jar with lid*
• water (enough to fill the baby food jar)
• multicolored glitter
• small lump of polymer modeling clay (try Fimo™ or Sculpey™ brands)
• white Styrofoam™ plate (9" [22.86 cm] diameter) (Seven students can share one.)
• black ink pen (waterproof)
• newspapers
• shallow bowls
• scissors

■ Tell the Class

"Snowflakes are fun to watch fall from the sky. Every single snowflake that falls is different from any other snowflake. Isn't that amazing? And even if snowflakes don't have any taste, they're fun to try to catch on your tongue!

Today you can draw a little picture of a snowman and place it inside a jar filled with water and glitter.

When you shake it, the glitter will spin around and look like snow. This way you can keep a little bit of winter with you throughout the whole year!"

■ How to Make It

For Teachers, Aides and Parent Volunteers

A. Use a pencil to trace a milk jug lid onto a white Styrofoam™ plate. You should be able to trace about seven circles onto a plate. Every student will need one circle.

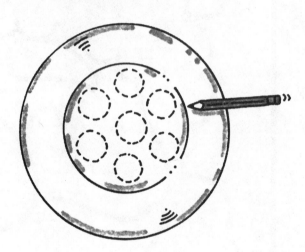

B. Fill shallow bowls with multicolored glitter. Put a teaspoon in each bowl. Students can share the bowls (three per bowl). Place the bowls on newspapers.

■ How to Make It

For Students

1. Use the black ink pen to draw a snowman onto the Styrofoam™ circle. (Older students can get a bit more elaborate if they like.)

2. Press the lump of polymer clay into the center of the baby food jar lid (rim up). Put your snowman drawing into the lump of clay so that it stands up.

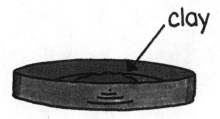

clay

3. Put a teaspoon of glitter into the baby food jar and fill it with water almost to the top. (Younger students will need assistance.)

glitter

4. Carefully screw the lid onto the jar. Trim your snowman circle with scissors if it's too large to fit in the jar. Make sure it is on very tight! Ask your teacher to make sure your lid is on tight enough. (Younger students will need assistance.)

5. Shake the jar up and down for a little while. Then set it upside down, as shown, and watch the pieces of glitter until they all stop moving.

6. Take your snow globe home. Whenever you feel like watching the snow fall, just shake it up!

Valentine Jar

■ Perfect Timing

Make this craft when studying winter, Valentine's Day or when reading:

- *Happy Valentine's Day, Emma!* James Stevenson. Greenwillow Books, 1987.
- *A Sweetheart for Valentine.* Lorna Balian. Abingdon, 1979.
- *Nelson in Love: An Adam Joshua Valentine's Story.* Janice Lee Smith, HarperCollins, 1992.

■ Materials Needed

- small glass baby food jar with lid*
- piece of white yarn
- supply of wrapped candies, stickers, erasers, etc. (Each child will need to have enough to fill his jar. To help with the cost you may want to ask for a small amount of money from each child.)
- reproducible heart patterns
- red spray paint
- red tissue paper
- pink crayon
- red fine-tipped washable marker
- pencil
- glue
- shallow bowl

■ Tell the Class

"Valentine's Day is a good time to tell someone you

love how special they are to you. Sometimes we even give that person a little gift.

I'll show you how to make something that you can give to your valentine."

■ How to Make It

For Teachers, Aides and Parent Volunteers

A. Spray each student's jar lid (the outside of it) with red spray paint. Let it dry overnight. Do this step the day before you make this craft.

B. Put glue with a little bit of water into shallow bowls that students can share (two students per bowl).

C. Cut 15" (38.1 cm) pieces of white yarn. Each student will need one piece.

D. Photocopy the heart patterns for each student.

■ How to Make It

For Students

1. Color the heart pattern that says *Be Mine* with a pink crayon. Don't color the plain heart. Cut both hearts out.

2. Use a pencil to trace the plain heart on red tissue paper. Trace four hearts and cut them out.

3. Dip the tissue paper hearts into the glue mixture. Place them around the outside of the jar. Let them dry.

4. Glue the *Be Mine* heart to the red lid as shown.

5. Wait for your teacher to come around and fill your jar with goodies. Then screw on the lid and tie the white piece of yarn around the jar.

6. Decide who you'll be giving this special valentine's treat to.

Wonderful Kwanzaa Harvest

■ Perfect Timing

Make this craft when studying winter, Kwanzaa or when reading:

- *Snow Day.* Betsy Maestro. Crowell, 1986.
- *The Jacket I Wear in the Snow.* Shirley Neitzel. Greenwillow Books, 1989.
- *The First Snowfall.* Anne & Harlow Rockwell. Macmillan, 1987.

■ Materials Needed

- Styrofoam™ cup*
- green, red and black crayons or washable markers
- soft modeling dough

■ Tell the Class

"How many of you know what Kwanzaa is? It's a holiday that honors the cultural roots of African Americans. It starts on December 26 and lasts until January 1. During this time candles are lit, gifts are given, and seven special principles of living are talked about. Feasting is also part of the Kwanzaa celebration. An important symbol of this holiday is *mazao*—which are fruits and vegetables. They stand for the rewards of working together.

Today, in honor of Kwanzaa, we'll make pretend fruits and vegetables. Then we'll make a bowl, decorated with the colors of Kwanzaa (green, red and black) to put them in."

■ How to Make It

For Teachers, Aides and Parent Volunteers

Carefully cut Styrofoam™ cups in half. Every student will need one.

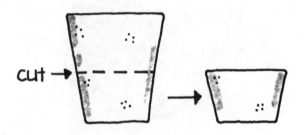

■ How to Make It

For Students

1. Use soft modeling dough to make small, pretend fruits. Some ideas are apples, oranges and bananas.

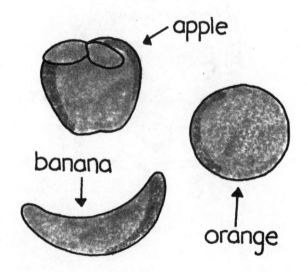

2. Use more soft modeling dough to make small, pretend vegetables. Some ideas are carrots, corn and lettuce.

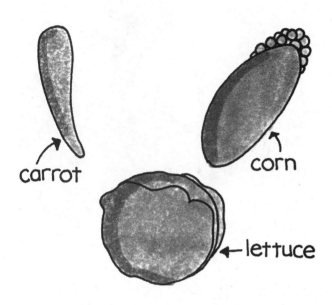

carrot

corn

← lettuce

3. Decorate the Styrofoam™ cup using the colors green, red and black. This is the bowl.

4. Put your pretend fruits and vegetables into the bowl.

5. Take your Kwanzaa basket home and display it for family members. Tell them about the Kwanzaa holiday.

Breezy Butterfly

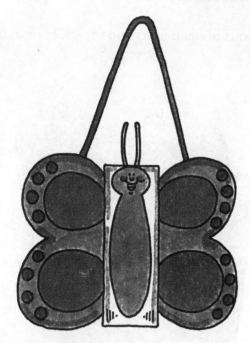

Today we'll make a pretend butterfly that can hang from a tree branch and swing back and forth in the breezes that blow by."

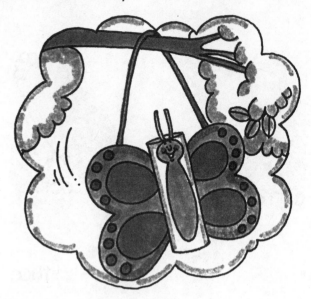

■ Perfect Timing

Make this craft when studying spring or reading:

* *The Butterfly That Stamped.* Rudyard Kipling. Bedrick Books, 1988.
* *Spring: Discovering the Seasons.* Lois Santrey. Troll Associates, 1983.
* *First Comes Spring.* Anne Rockwell. T.Y. Crowell, 1985.

■ Materials Needed

* toilet tissue tube*
* reproducible butterfly patterns (page 38)
* 2 pieces of yellow pipe cleaner
* masking tape
* piece of yarn
* crayons or washable markers
* yellow piece of construction paper
* glue
* scissors

■ Tell the Class

"When the season of spring arrives, it usually brings warm temperatures. The grass is green, flowers bloom and butterflies sail through the air.

■ How to Make It

For Teachers, Aides and Parent Volunteers

A. Photocopy the butterfly patterns (page 38) for every student.

B. Cut yellow pipe cleaners in half. Every student will need two halves.

C. Cut 22" (55.88 cm) pieces of yarn. Every student will need one piece.

D. Cut 4½" x 5¾" (11.43 x 14.61 cm) pieces of yellow construction paper. Each student will need one piece.

■ How to Make It

For Students

1. Glue the yellow construction paper around the toilet tissue tube. Put pieces of masking tape on the seam to make it extra secure.

masking tape

2. Color and cut out the butterfly pattern pieces. Use your imagination to decorate the wings.

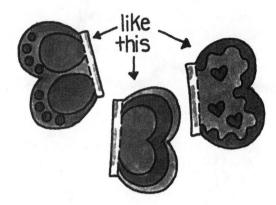

like this

3. Glue the butterfly head and body piece onto the tube.

4. Use masking tape to put the pipe cleaner pieces on the inside of the toilet tissue tube behind the head as shown. (Younger students will need assistance.)

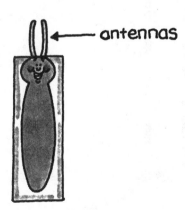

antennas

5. Fold the wings on the dotted lines and glue one onto each side of the tube. Secure with pieces of masking tape. (Younger students will need assistance.)

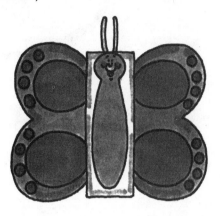

6. Use masking tape to secure the piece of yarn onto the back of the wings as shown.

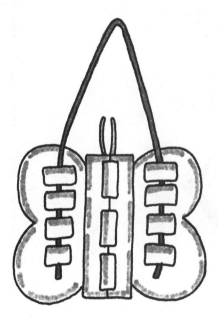

7. Have your mom or dad hang your butterfly from a tree branch where you can watch it swing in the wind.

Butterfly Patterns

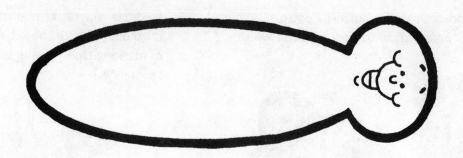

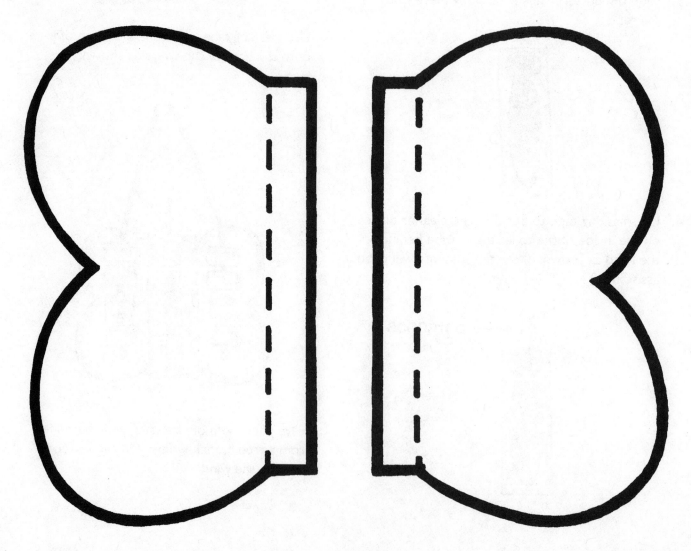

Bunny Basket

■ Perfect Timing

Make this craft when studying spring, Easter or when reading:

• *Silly Tilly and the Easter Bunny.* Lillian Hoban. Harper & Row, 1987.
• *Little Rabbit's Easter Surprise.* Kenn and Joanne Compton. Holiday House, 1992.
• *Happy Easter, Little Critter.* Mercer Mayer. Western Publishing Co., 1988.

■ Materials Needed

• plastic milk jug* (gallon size)
• reproducible bunny pattern (page 41)
• washable markers or crayons
• white shirt box cardboard*
• tape
• pencil
• glue
• scissors

■ Tell the Class

"Have you noticed more birds outside lately? How about bunnies? During springtime the animals are busy buiding and repairing nests to make homes for their babies.

You're going to make a special Bunny Basket that can be a home for some of your things, maybe toys or crayons or colored pencils."

■ How to Make It

For Teachers, Aides and Parent Volunteers

A. Photocopy the bunny patterns (page 41) for every student.

B. Cut the sides off of white shirt boxes. You'll be left with rectangles of shirt box cardboard. Every student will need one piece.

C. Carefully cut off the top of a one-gallon plastic milk jug as shown. Every student will need one.

keep handle

(side view)

■ How to Make It

For Students

1. Cut out the bunny ear pattern and use a pencil to trace it onto the shirt box cardboard to make two ears. Cut them out.

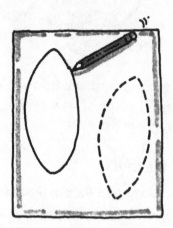

2. Draw the insides of the ears as shown and color them pink.

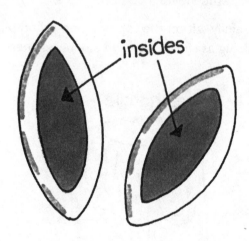

insides

3. Color all the other bunny pattern pieces and cut them out.

4. Glue the eyes and nose piece onto the milk jug as shown. Secure the nose piece with tape.

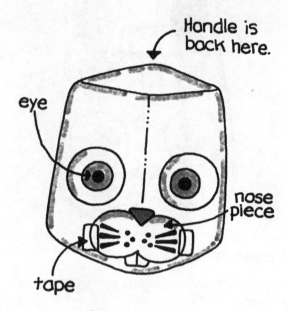

Handle is back here.

eye

nose piece

tape

5. Tape the ears onto the milk jug as shown.

6. The night before Easter put some Easter grass in your basket. Leave it out so the Easter Bunny can place treats in it!

Bunny Patterns

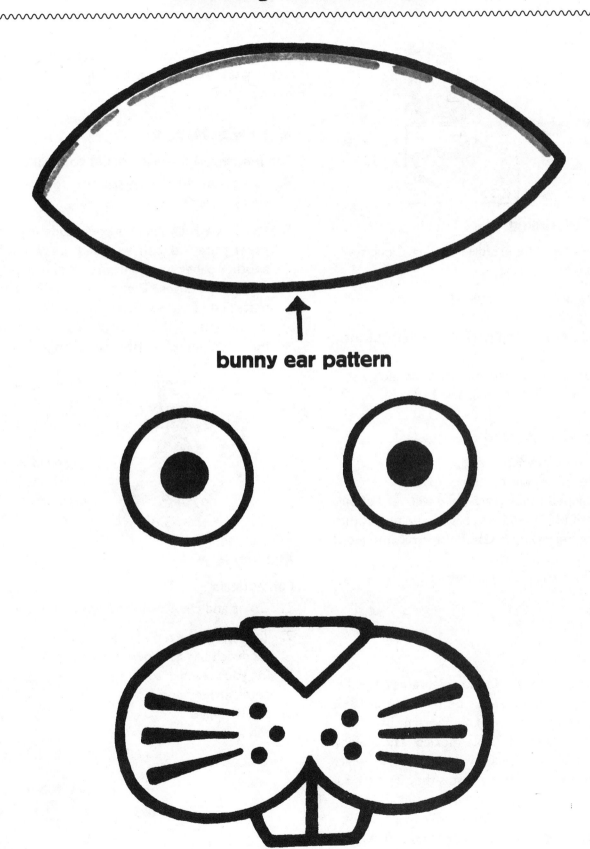

↑
bunny ear pattern

Easy Donkey Piñata

■ Perfect Timing

Make this craft when studying spring, Cinco de Mayo or when reading:

- *Have You Seen Birds?* Joanne Oppenheim. Scholastic Inc., 1986.
- *My Spring Robin.* Ann Rockwell. Scholastic Inc., 1989.
- *Weather.* Gillimard Jeunesse and Pascale de Bourgoing. Scholastic Inc., 1989.

■ Materials Needed

- zip-to-seal sandwich bag*
- reproducible donkey patterns (page 44)
- soft wrapped candy (Each child will need enough to fill half of his sandwich bag. To help with the cost, you may want to ask for a small amount of money from each child.)
- crayons or washable markers
- tape
- scissors

■ Tell the Class

"Each year on May 5, Mexico celebrates a holiday called *Cinco de Mayo*. It was on that date, in 1862, that a Mexican army won an important battle against the French at Puebla, Mexico. The Mexican people celebrate this day by having fiestas—which are like festivals. At these fiestas they have parades, fireworks, food, dances and piñatas. Piñatas are often animal-shaped containers filled with candy and other goodies. They are hung up and children break them open with sticks.

Let's celebrate Cinco de Mayo by making easy donkey piñatas. When you are finished, I will put candy in it for you."

■ How to Make It

For Teachers, Aides and Parent Volunteers

A. Photocopy the donkey patterns (page 44) for every student.

B. Make a parrot piñata for your students! Fill a paper plate with soft, wrapped candy. Place another paper plate on top of it and staple around the edges. Then photocopy the parrot pattern on page 43. Color it, cut it out and glue it onto one of the paper plates. Paper-punch a hole through both plates and string a long piece of yarn through it. Knot the ends of the yarn together to make a hanger. Hang it up and let the children take turns trying to break it open with a Whiffle™ bat.

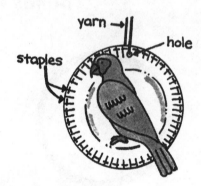

■ How to Make It

For Students

1. Color and cut out the donkey patterns.

2. Tape the pattern pieces onto the zip-to-seal sandwich bag as shown to make a piñata. Wait for your teacher to come around and put wrapped candy in it.

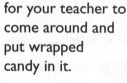
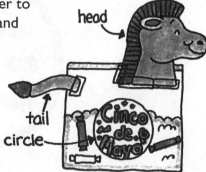

Parrot Patterns

TLC10027 Copyright © Teaching & Learning Company, Carthage, IL 62321

Donkey Patterns

Lazy Daisy Bookmark

I imagine that you'll enjoy doing all kinds of things outdoors this spring. Have you ever read a book outside? Let's make a bookmark today to celebrate the season of spring. It'll come in handy when you need to remember your spot in a book."

■ How to Make It

For Teachers, Aides and Parent Volunteers

A. Use pinking shears to cut out 2¾" x 7½" (6.99 x 19.05 cm) pieces of denim. Every student will need one piece.

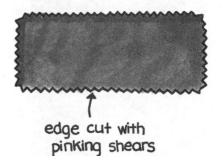

edge cut with pinking shears

B. Photocopy the flower patterns. Cut them out and trace onto felt. Use white felt for the petals, green felt for the leaves and yellow felt for the center. Every student will need one petal pattern, two leaves and one center pattern.

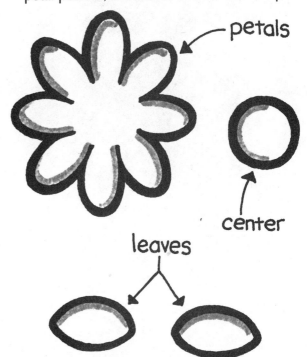

petals

center

leaves

■ Perfect Timing

Make this craft when studying spring or when reading:

- *One Step, Two*— Charlotte Zolotow. Lothrop, Lee & Shepard Books, 1981.
- *Planting a Rainbow.* Lois Ehlert. Harcourt Brace Jovanovich, 1988.
- *Alison's Zinnia.* Arnold Lobel. Greenwillow Books, 1984.

■ Materials Needed

- piece of denim material from a pair of blue jeans*
- pinking shears (scissors that cut a zigzag design)
- reproducible flower patterns
- scraps of white, green and yellow felt
- piece of green yarn
- washable, black fine-tipped marker
- glue
- scissors

■ Tell the Class

"Spring is a wonderful season! It's as if nature is waking up after a long nap! The sky becomes bluer, the grass turns green and flowers bloom all around us.

C. Cut 3" (7.62) pieces of green yarn. Every student will need one piece.

■ How to Make It

For Students

1. Place your piece of denim so the light side is faceup. Then arrange the flower pattern pieces and piece of yarn as shown. Glue everything in place.

2. Use the washable, black fine-tipped marker to write your name at the bottom. Draw a smiling face on the center and add details to the leaves.

3. Keep your Lazy Daisy Bookmark handy so you can use it to mark your spot in your favorite books.

Lion and Lamb Necklace

■ Perfect Timing

Make this craft when studying spring, the month of March, the letter *L* or when reading:

- *The Happy Lion.* Louise Fatio. McGraw-Hill, 1954.
- *Dandelion.* Don Freeman. Viking, 1964.
- *Sheep in a Jeep.* Nancy Shaw. Houghton Mifflin, 1986.

■ Materials Needed

- frozen juice lid* (12 oz. [354.9 ml])
- crayons
- piece of yarn
- yellow yarn scraps
- 2 cotton balls
- reproducible lion and lamb patterns (page 49)
- tape
- glue
- scissors

■ Tell the Class

"There is an old saying about the weather in the month of March. It says, 'If it comes in like a lion, it goes out like a lamb.' This means if March starts out being very fierce like a lion with lots of wind

and snow, then it will end gently like a lamb with light breezes and warm temperatures. Of course, this doesn't always happen. But it's fun to see if it does.

Today we're going to make a special necklace that you can wear during the month of March. Each day you will look at the weather and then decide if you should wear it with the lion or the lamb picture showing."

■ How to Make It

For Teachers, Aides and Parent Volunteers

A. Photocopy the lion and lamb patterns page (page 49). Cut out on the dotted lines to make three strips. Each student will need one strip.

B. Cut 36" (91.44 cm) pieces of yarn. Each student will need one piece.

■ How to Make It

For Students

1. Color and cut out the lion and lamb patterns.

2. Knot the ends of the piece of yarn together. Tape it onto the juice lid as shown. (Younger students will need assistance.)

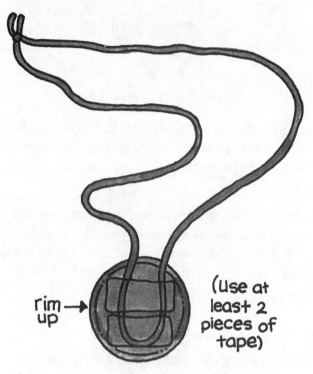

rim up →

(Use at least 2 pieces of tape)

3. Glue the lion pattern onto one side of the lid and the lamb pattern onto the other. Tape the sides of the patterns on to make them extra secure.

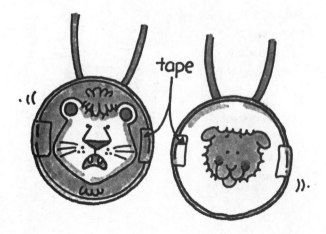

tape

4. Tear the two cotton balls apart and glue the pieces around the lamb's face.

5. Glue bits of yellow yarn onto the lion's mane.

6. Look out the window to see if you should wear your necklace on the lion side or the lamb side.

Lion and Lamb Patterns

TLC10027 Copyright © Teaching & Learning Company, Carthage, IL 62321

Miniature Keen Kite

Today I'll show you how to make a miniature kite. When we are finished with our kites, we'll hang them from our classroom lights."

■ How to Make It

For Teachers, Aides and Parent Volunteers

A. Make photocopies of the kite patterns (page 52) for every student.

B. Cut 12" (30.48 cm) pieces of yarn. Every student will need two pieces.

■ How to Make It

For Students

1. Color and cut out all kite pattern pieces. Use your imagination to decorate the bows.

2. Glue the two craft sticks onto the back of the kite as shown. Let them dry. Add pieces of tape to secure their positions. Write your name on the edge of the kite.

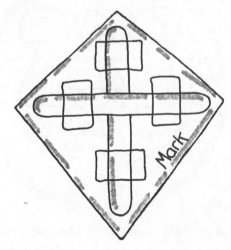

■ Perfect Timing

Make this craft when studying spring or when reading:

- *The Kite.* Mary Packard. Childrens Press, 1989.
- *The Big Kite Contest.* Dortha Ruthstrom. Pantheon Books, 1980.
- *Rabbit's Birthday Kite.* Maryann McDonald. Bantam Books, 1991.

■ Materials Needed

- 2 craft sticks*
- reproducible kite patterns (page 52)
- 2 pieces of yarn
- markers or crayons
- tape
- glue
- scissors

■ Tell the Class

"One of the best things to do on a windy spring day is fly a kite. It's so exciting to let it climb higher and higher in the sky. And it's fun to watch its tail dance back and forth.

TLC10027 Copyright © Teaching & Learning Company, Carthage, IL 62321

3. Use bits of tape to attach the tail bows onto the shorter piece of yarn.

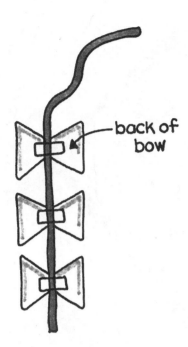

back of bow

4. Tape the tail onto the back of the kite.

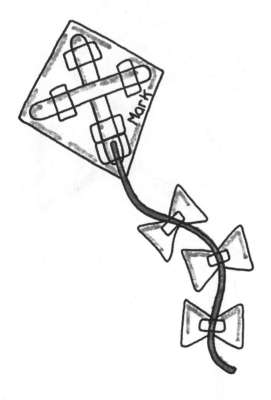

5. Tape the other piece of yarn onto the back of the kite as shown to create a hanger.

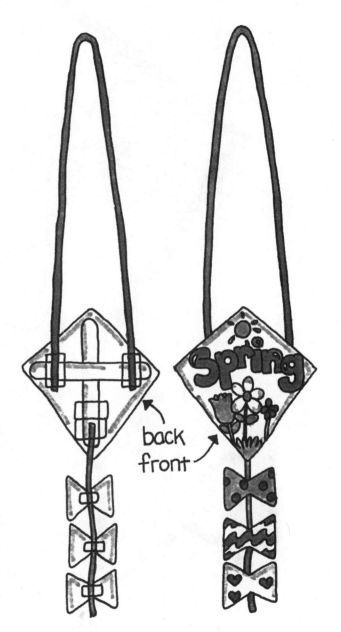

back
front

6. Let the teacher hang your kite from the lights where all your classmates can admire it.

Kite Patterns

Mother's Day Box

■ Perfect Timing

Make this craft when studying spring, as part of the Mother's Day celebration or when reading:

- *Hazel's Amazing Mother.* Rosemary Wells. Dial Books for Young Readers, 1981.
- *The Mother's Day Mice.* Eve Bunting. Clarion Books, 1986.
- *The Quiet Mother and the Noisy Little Boy.* Charlotte Zolotow. Harper & Row, 1989.

■ Materials Needed

- box with lid* (the kind that checks come in or any box that is similar in size)
- reproducible Mother's Day and coupon patterns (page 55)
- wrapping paper (ask parents to send pastel colored or flowered pieces)
- yarn and pieces of lace
- pencil
- tape
- washable markers or crayons
- glue
- scissors

■ Tell the Class

"Every year during the month of May we celebrate an occasion called Mother's Day. It's a day to tell and show our mothers (or someone who is like a mother) how much we love and appreciate them.

Let's make a pretty little box for your mother. You can fill it with coupons that tell what tasks you will do for her. I'm sure she'll love it!"

■ How to Make It

For Teachers, Aides and Parent Volunteers

Photocopy a Mother's Day and coupon patterns (page 55) for every student.

■ How to Make It

For Students

1. Cover the lid with wrapping paper. (Younger students will need assistance.)

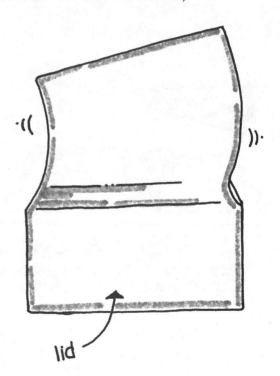

lid

2. Color the Mother's Day oval pattern. Write your name on the blank. Cut it and the coupons out.

3. Glue the Mother's Day oval pattern onto the lid as shown.

4. Decorate the lid by gluing on yarn and lace.

glue lace on the sides

5. Fill out the coupons with tasks such as *set the table*, *help fold laundry* or *feed the cat.* If you need to, ask your teacher for ideas. (Younger students will need assistance.)

6. Place the completed coupons inside the box and replace the lid.

7. Deliver it to your mom on Mother's Day with a big hug!

Mother's Day and Coupon Patterns

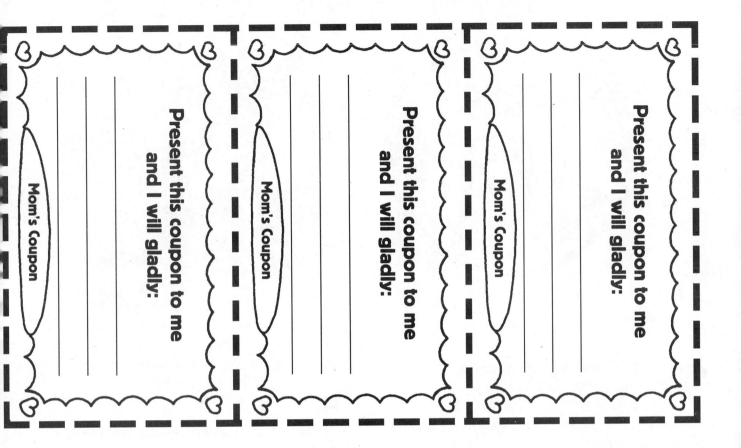

Present this coupon to me
and I will gladly:

Mom's Coupon

Present this coupon to me
and I will gladly:

Mom's Coupon

Present this coupon to me
and I will gladly:

Mom's Coupon

Happy Mother's Day

Love, _____

Big Hit Baseball Magnet

■ Perfect Timing

Make this craft when studying summer or when reading:

- *Frank and Ernest Play Ball.* Alexandra Day. Scholastic, 1990.
- *Max.* Rachel Isadora. Macmillan, 1976.
- *Here Comes the Strikeout.* Leonard P. Kessler. Harper & Row, 1965.

■ Materials Needed

- frozen juice lid* (12 oz. [354.9 ml])
- reproducible baseball pattern (page 58)
- 2 strips of self-sticking magnet (To help with the cost, you may want to ask for a small amount of money from each child.)
- red fine-tipped washable marker
- glue
- scissors

■ Tell the Class

"Summer is a great time to play and do lots of things. We can bike ride, rollerblade and swim. How many of you like to play baseball? Let's go outside and play a game! (If this is not possible, simply omit this sentence.)

When we come, in we'll make a magnet that looks like a baseball. When you're finished, you can take it home and put it on your refrigerator."

■ How to Make It

For Teachers, Aides and Parent Volunteers

A. Make photocopies of the baseball pattern. Cut on the dotted lines to make six patterns. Every student will need one pattern.

B. Cut 1¾" (4.45 cm) pieces of self-sticking magnet from a long strip. (You can buy this at craft stores.) Every student will need two pieces.

■ How to Make It

For Students

1. Color the baseball pattern. Use the red fine-tipped marker to trace over the stitching marks on the baseball. Fill in your name and then cut it out.

2. Glue the pattern onto the juice lid.

3. Put the pieces of self-sticking magnet onto the back of the lid.

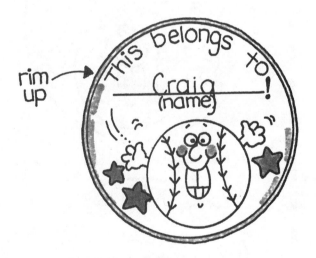

4. Take your magnet home. Use it to hold your art on the refrigerator door!

TLC10027 Copyright © Teaching & Learning Company, Carthage, IL 62321

Baseball Pattern

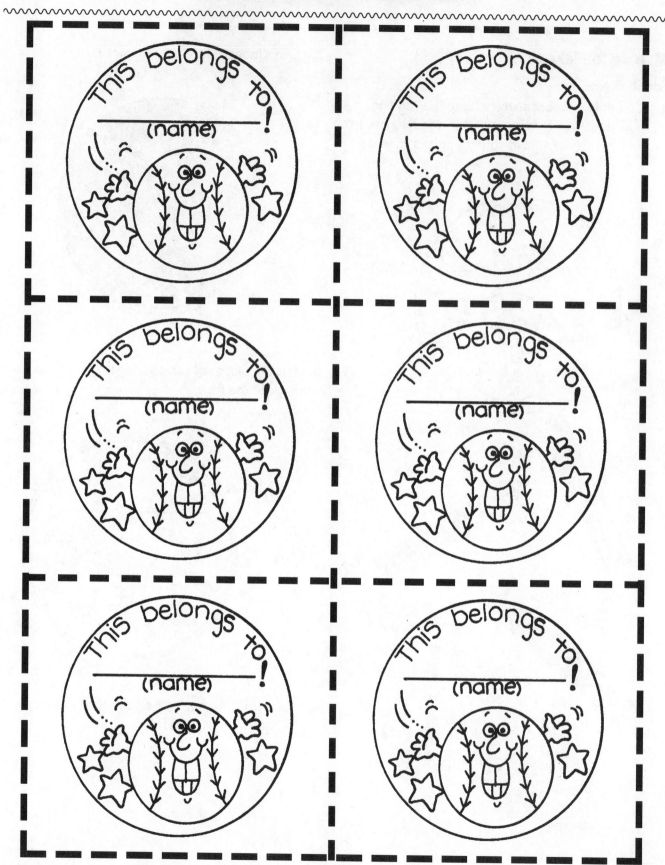

This belongs to!

_____
(name)

This belongs to!

_____
(name)

This belongs to!

_____
(name)

This belongs to!

_____
(name)

This belongs to!

_____
(name)

This belongs to!

_____
(name)

Camping Diorama

Perfect Timing

Make this craft when studying summer or when reading:

- *Where the River Begins.* Thomas Locker. Dial Books for Young Readers, 1985.
- *The Night We Slept Outside.* Anne F. Rockwell. Macmillan, 1983.
- *Do Not Disturb.* Nancy Tafuri. Greenwillow Books, 1989.

Materials Needed

- shoe box* (no lid)
- light blue and green construction paper
- tiny twigs
- tiny pebbles (or natural colored aquarium gravel)
- magazines* (with pictures of trees, bushes, etc.)
- tape
- piece of brown grocery bag*
- crayons or washable markers
- glue
- shallow bowls
- scissors

Tell the Class

"How many of you have ever been camping? Whether you sleep in a tent or a camper, it can be a great adventure.

Let's make a pretend campsite! You can decide what park or even state you are camping in. You will decide where the trees and bushes should be. And you'll even get to pitch a tent!"

How to Make It

For Teachers, Aides and Parent Volunteers

A. Gather some tiny twigs and tiny pebbles in a lunch bag. Place some in shallow bowls that students can share (three to a bowl).

B. Cut 5" x 6½" (12.7 x 16.51 cm) pieces from large brown grocery bags. Every student will need one piece.

C. Write the words *Camping Diorama* on the chalkboard.

How to Make It

For Students

1. Use crayons or washable markers to write your name with an *apostrophe s* and the words *Camping Diorama* (they are written on the chalkboard for you to copy) onto a piece of paper. (Younger students will need assistance.) Cut it out and tape it to the long side of the shoe box.

2. Cut out and then glue pieces of light blue construction paper to cover the inside back and side panels of the shoe box as shown. This will be the sky. (Younger students will need assistance.)

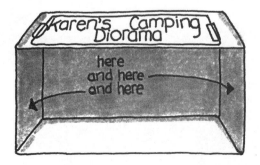

3. Cut out and then glue a piece of green construction paper onto the remaining inside shoe box panel as shown. This will be the grass. (Younger students will need assistance.)

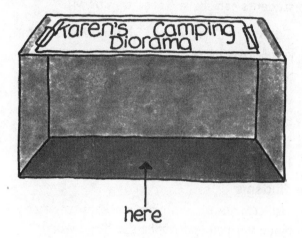

here

4. Cut out pictures of trees and bushes from magazines. Glue them onto the light blue background to create a landscape.

5. Place your grocery bag piece horizontally. Fold it in half and then unfold it. Then fold in the left and right edges about ½" (1.27 cm) as shown. Glue these edges down onto the green construction paper to create a tent. (Younger students will need assistance.)

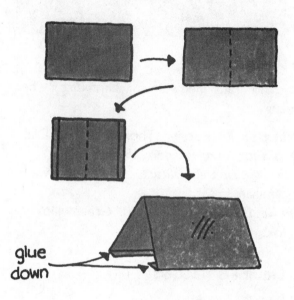

glue down

6. Glue tiny pebbles into a circle shape onto the green construction paper to create a campfire site. Glue tiny twigs inside the pebbles to look like firewood.

Cute Clown Crayon Carrier

■ Perfect Timing

Make this craft when studying summer, the circus or when reading:

- *The Clown-Arounds Go on Vacation.* John N. Cole. Parents Magazine Press, 1983.
- *You Think It's Fun to Be a Clown!* David A. Adler. Doubleday, 1980.
- *C Is for Clown.* Stan and Jan Berenstain. Random House, 1972.

■ Materials Needed

- bleach jug* (white, gallon size—cleaned and rinsed with hot water)
- piece of red butcher paper
- scraps of red and blue construction paper
- piece of white yarn
- pencil
- black washable marker
- red washable marker
- tape
- glue
- scissors

■ Tell the Class

"There are lots of fun things you can do during summer vacation. No doubt you'll enjoy playing with your friends at the park and at each other's homes. When you're looking for something to do, don't forget coloring!

I'll show you how to make a container that looks like a clown. Keep your crayons in it when it's finished."

■ How to Make It

For Teachers, Aides and Parent Volunteers

A. Carefully cut the bottom portion (measuring 4½" [11.43 cm] high) off of clean bleach jug.

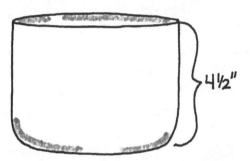

Then paper-punch two holes (directly across from each other) ½" (1.27 cm) down from the top edge. Every student will need a container prepared like this.

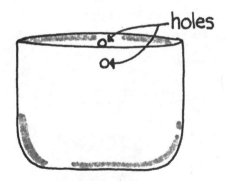

B. Cut 2½" x 13" (6.35 x 33.02 cm) pieces of red butcher paper. Every student will need one piece.

C. Cut 18" (45.72 cm) pieces of white yarn. Every student will need one piece.

TLC10027 Copyright © Teaching & Learning Company, Carthage, IL 62321

■ How to Make It

For Students

1. Cut two small circles from scraps of blue construction paper. Use the black washable marker to make a small circle in the center of each. These are the eyes. Cut one small circle (slightly larger than the blue ones) from a scrap of red construction paper. This is the nose.

2. Position the red piece of butcher paper horizontally. Then use scissors to "fringe" the bottom edges halfway up as shown. This is the hair. (Younger students will need assistance.)

3. Starting a little before the punched hole on the right, glue the hair around the container (about 1¼" [3.18 cm] down from the top edge). Secure each of the ends and the middle with tape.

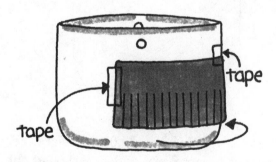

4. Glue the eyes and nose onto your container as shown.

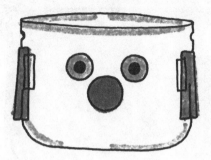

5. Use the red washable marker to draw a smiling mouth onto the container.

6. Thread the piece of yarn through the punched holes. Then tie and knot the ends as shown. (Younger students will need assistance.)

Ocean Felt Board

■ Perfect Timing

Make this craft when studying summer, the ocean or when reading:

- *Under the Water.* Harriet Ziefert. Viking, 1990.
- *Otto Is Different.* Franz Bradenberg. Greenwillow Books, 1985.
- *Summer: Discovering the Seasons.* Lois Santrey. Troll Associates, 1983.

■ Materials Needed

- Styrofoam™ tray* (7⅛" x 9¼" [18.1 x 23.5 cm]—any color)
- piece of light blue felt
- green yarn scraps
- reproducible ocean items patterns (page 65)
- felt scraps
- washable, fine-tipped markers
- masking tape
- various colors of sequins
- glue
- scissors

■ Tell the Class

"Going to the beach is a great way to cool down on a hot summer day! You can build sand castles, and of course, play and swim in the water.

Today you'll get to make a felt board on which you can arrange different things from the ocean. When you're done, use your imagination to make up a story that tells about all the items on your felt board."

■ How Make It

For Teachers, Aides and Parent Volunteers

Photocopy the ocean items patterns (page 65) for every student.

■ How to Make It

For Students

1. Cut the light blue felt to fit the inside of your Styrofoam™ tray. (Younger students will need assistance.) Glue into place.

TLC10027 Copyright © Teaching & Learning Company, Carthage, IL 62321

2. Cut all the patterns out. Put loops of masking tape on the backs of the items and press them onto felt. Cut around the patterns. Remove the paper patterns and discard. (Younger students will need assistance.)

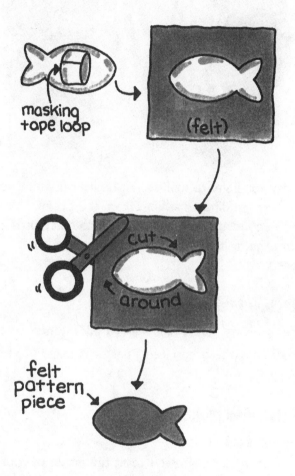

3. Use washable, fine-tipped markers to draw details on the felt pieces.

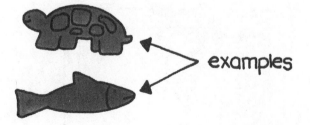

examples

4. Glue colored sequins to the coral pieces. Glue green yarn to the seaweed piece.

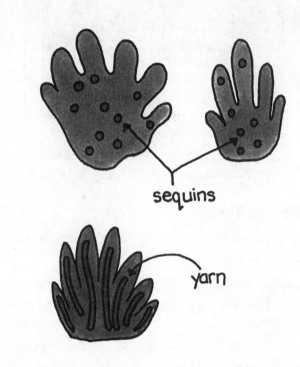

5. Pretend you are a scuba diver. What do you think you might see? Arrange the ocean items onto your felt board to make different scenes.

Ocean Items Patterns

Snappy Sailboat

■ Perfect Timing

Make this craft when studying summer, sailboats or when reading:

- *Sailing to the Sea.* Mary Claire Helldorfer. Viking 1991.
- *Summer on Cleo's Island.* Natalie G. Sylvester. Farrar, Straus, 1977.
- *There and Back Again.* Harold Jones. Atheneum, 1977.

■ Materials Needed

- lunch bag* (Two students can share one.)
- reproducible sail and sailor patterns (page 68)
- drinking straw*
- scraps of construction paper, felt, material and yarn
- gold and silver glitter
- small photo of child's face that can be cut out and used for this craft
- washable markers or crayons
- tape
- glue
- shallow bowls
- scissors

■ Tell the Class

"During the summer it's lots of fun to watch sail-

boats. The sails come in all different colors and with interesting designs on them.

Would you like to design the sails of your very own sailboat? That's just what you'll get to do today! Let's get started!"

■ How to Make It

For Teachers, Aides and Parent Volunteers

A. Photocopy the sail and sailor patterns (page 68) for every student.

B. Cover a bulletin board or an area of wall with blue paper. Use a marker to draw "waves" onto it. Title it "Snappy Sailboats." Display all the finished sailboats on this ocean.

C. Put gold or silver glitter into shallow bowls that students can share (three students per bowl).

■ How to Make It

For Students

1. Cut out the front and back panels of a lunch sack. Give one panel to another student to use. (Younger students will need assistance.)

2. Place your lunch bag panel horizontally (sideways). Fold it in half as shown. Fold both ends in and tape down as shown. Flip it over. This is the boat. (Younger students will need assistance.)

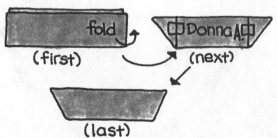

TLC10027 Copyright © Teaching & Learning Company, Carthage, IL 62321

3. Cut out the sail pattern (do not cut it apart). Use your imagination to decorate the sail with washable markers or crayons and the materials provided (construction paper, felt, glitter, etc.).

4. Tape the drinking straw onto the line between the sails.

5. Tape the drinking straw onto the inside back panel of the boat as shown.

6. Cut out and color the sailor pattern. Cut out your face from your photo and glue it onto the sailor's blank face.

7. Glue the sailor onto the inside front panel of the boat as shown.

8. Give your completed sailboat to your teacher so she can display it. Tell your teacher where you would sail and why if you were really a sailor. (For example, "I'd go the Hawaii because I want to see a palm tree!")

Sail and Sailor Patterns

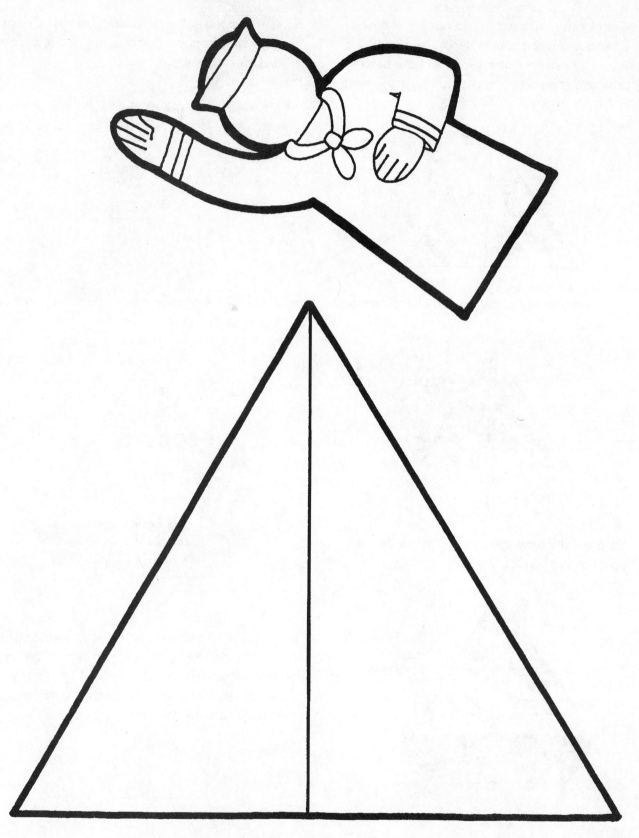

Tribute Tie to Dad

■ Perfect Timing

Make this craft when studying summer, Father's Day or when reading:

- *Daddy Has a Pair of Striped Shorts.* Mimi Otey. Farrar, Straus and Giroux, 1990.
- *A Perfect Father's Day.* Eve Bunting. Clarion Books, 1991.
- *Daddy Makes the Best Spaghetti.* Anna Grossnickle Hines. Clarion Books, 1986.

■ Materials Needed

- large brown grocery bag* (Six students can share one.)
- reproducible tie pattern and poem (page 71)
- tissue paper scraps
- construction paper scraps
- piece of yarn
- washable markers or crayons
- pencil
- newspapers
- glitter
- tape
- shallow bowls
- glue
- scissors

■ Tell the Class

"Every year Father's Day is celebrated in the month of June. On that day we treat our dads (or someone like a dad) extra special! There are lots of things we can do to show our dad how much we appreciate him. We can help plan his favorite breakfast, bring him his slippers and give him plenty of hugs.

Today you'll get to make a Tribute Tie for Dad to wear on Father's Day. When he reads the poem that you've glued onto it, he'll know how much you love him!"

■ How to Make It

For Teachers, Aides and Parent Volunteers

A. Photocopy a tie pattern (page 71) for every student.

B. Cut 30" (76.2 cm) pieces of yarn. Every student will need one piece.

C. Put any color glitter into shallow bowls that students can share (three students per bowl). Place the bowls on newspapers.

■ How to Make It

For Students

1. Cut the front, back and side panels out of a large brown grocery bag. Cut the front and back panels in half (horizontally). Keep one piece for yourself and give the rest to five other classmates. (Younger students will need assistance.)

2. Cut out the tie pattern and use a pencil to trace it onto the piece of grocery bag. Cut it out.

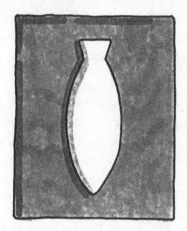

3. Cut out the poem. Glue it onto the tie as shown.

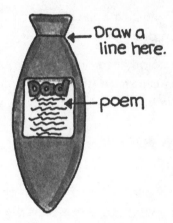

Draw a line here.

poem

4. Cut different sized hearts out of tissue paper and construction paper scraps. Glue them onto the tie.

5. Smear glue onto the word *Dad*. Put glitter on it and shake off the extra onto the newspapers.

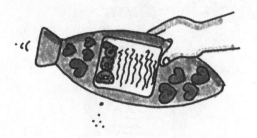

6. Tape the yarn onto the tie as shown.

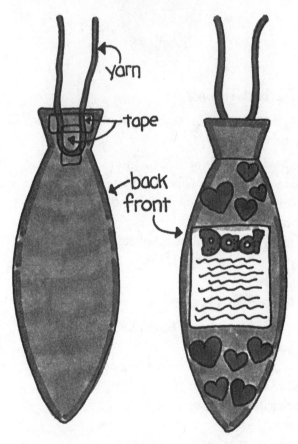

yarn

tape

back

front

7. Give this tie to your dad the morning of Father's Day. Have him wear it around his neck. Tell him you made it for him because you love him a lot.

Neck Tie Pattern

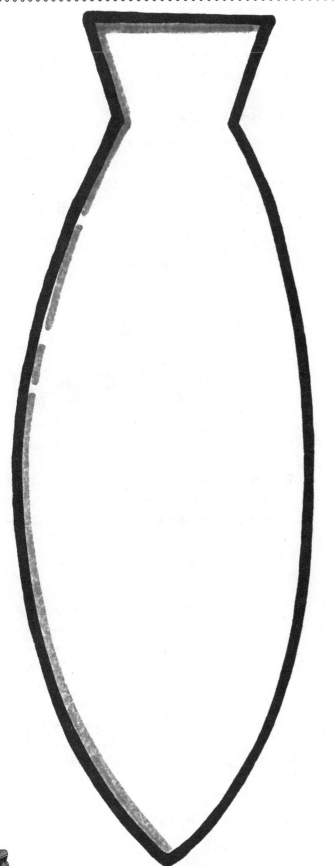

Dad

Dad, there's no one quite
    like you.
I appreciate the things
    you do.
I love you lots and that
    is why,
I made for you this
    Tribute Tie.

Wacky Napkin Rings

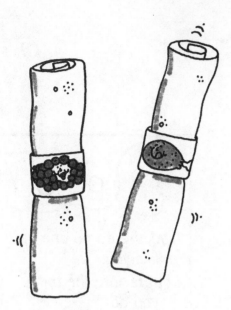

Today we'll make special rings that you can slide rolled-up napkins into. Take them with you whenever you and your family go for a picnic."

■ How to Make It

For Teachers, Aides and Parent Volunteers

A. Make photocopies of the food items patterns (page 73). Cut on the dotted lines to make two halves. Every student will need one half.

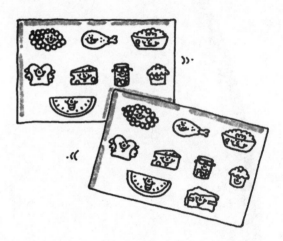

■ Perfect Timing

Make this craft when studying summer or when reading:

- *Really Eager and the Glorious Watermelon Contest.* Richard E. Cheney. Dutton, 1970.
- *A Summer Day.* Douglas Florian. Greenwillow Books, 1988.
- *When Summer Ends.* Susi Gregg Fowler. Greenwillow Books, 1989.

B. Cut the backs off of used envelopes. Mark off 1" (2.54 cm) segments on both sides and draw straight lines across. You'll need to use envelopes large enough so that you'll end up with nine segments.

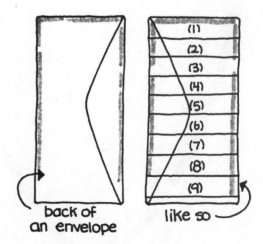

back of an envelope

like so

(1) (2) (3) (4) (5) (6) (7) (8) (9)

■ Materials Needed

- white used envelopes*
- reproducible food items patterns (page 73)
- 9 paper napkins
- tape
- markers or crayons
- glue
- scissors

■ Tell the Class

"Because the weather is so warm during the summer, people like to go on picnics. You can have a picnic at a park, at the beach or even in your own backyard. You could even have a picnic and invite your stuffed animals to be your guests.

■ How to Make It

For Students

1. Cut on the lines on the envelope to end up with nine strips.

2. Color the food items patterns and cut everything out. Glue a food item onto the middle of each strip.

3. Form the strips into circles and tape them together. (Younger students will need assistance.)

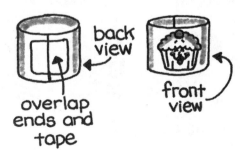

back view

front view

overlap ends and tape

4. Roll up a napkin and slide it into each ring.

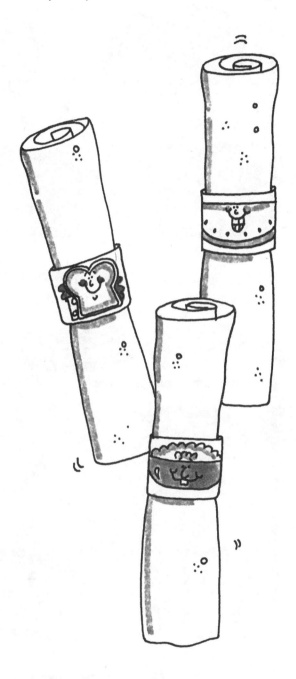

5. Take them all home. Next time you and your family go on a picnic, tell everyone you'll bring the napkins!

Food Items Patterns

Save 'n' Send

~~~~~~

Dear Parent or Guardian:

We will be making crafts that use recyclable household items. Would you please help by sending the following circled items to school (cleaned and rinsed if necessary) with your child?

baby food jars (small, glass with lids)
bacon plastic sheets (found inside bacon packages)
bleach jug (white, gallon size, cleaned and rinsed with hot water)
boxes with lids (that checks come in—3½" x 6½" by 1½" [8.89 x 16.51 x 3.81 cm])
cardboard cereal boxes (flattened)
cardboard shirt boxes (white)
cardboard shoe boxes (no lids)
craft sticks (from frozen treats)
denim material from old blue jeans

drinking straws (rinsed thoroughly)
envelopes (white and used)
fabric scraps: felt (white and other colors), burlap
frozen juice cans (12 oz. [354.9 ml])
frozen juice can lids (12 oz. [354.9 ml])
grocery bags (large and brown)
laundry detergent caps (that fit inside 12 oz. [354.9 ml] frozen juice cans)
lunch bags (not soiled)
magazines (with pictures of people)
magazines (with pictures of trees, bushes, etc.)

men's or women's white or light colored button-up shirts
peanut butter jar lids (1 lb. 2 oz. [504 g])
plastic milk jugs (gallon size)
Styrofoam™ cups
Styrofoam™ trays (white)
toilet tissue tubes
tuna cans
zip-to-seal sandwich bags (not soiled)
other: _____
_____

If you have any questions, please feel free to call me. Thank you very much! I appreciate your cooperation!

Sincerely,

_____   _____   _____
(teacher's name)   (school's phone number)   (date)

~~~~~~

 # Sufficiently Stocked

~~~~~~

Dear Parent or Guardian:

Thank you very much for sending recyclable household items to school with your child to use for crafts. We now have plenty of the following circled items. You will no longer need to send them.

baby food jars (small, glass with lids)
bacon plastic sheets (found inside bacon packages)
bleach jug (white, gallon size, cleaned and rinsed with hot water)
boxes with lids (that checks come in—3½" x 6½" by 1½" [8.89 x 16.51 x 3.81 cm])
cardboard cereal boxes (flattened)
cardboard shirt boxes (white)
cardboard shoe boxes (no lids)
craft sticks (from frozen treats)
denim material from old blue jeans

drinking straws (rinsed thoroughly)
envelopes (white and used)
fabric scraps: felt (white and other colors), burlap
frozen juice cans (12 oz. [354.9 ml])
frozen juice can lids (12 oz. [354.9 ml])
grocery bags (large and brown)
laundry detergent caps (that fit inside 12 oz. [354.9 ml] frozen juice cans)
lunch bags (not soiled)
magazines (with pictures of people)
magazines (with pictures of trees, bushes, etc.)

men's or women's white or light colored button-up shirts
peanut butter jar lids (1 lb. 2 oz. [504 g])
plastic milk jugs (gallon size)
Styrofoam™ cups
Styrofoam™ trays (white)
toilet tissue tubes
tuna cans
zip-to-seal sandwich bags (not soiled)
other: _____
_____

If you have any questions, please feel free to call me. Thank you very much! I appreciate your cooperation!

Sincerely,

_____   _____   _____
(teacher's name)   (school's phone number)   (date)

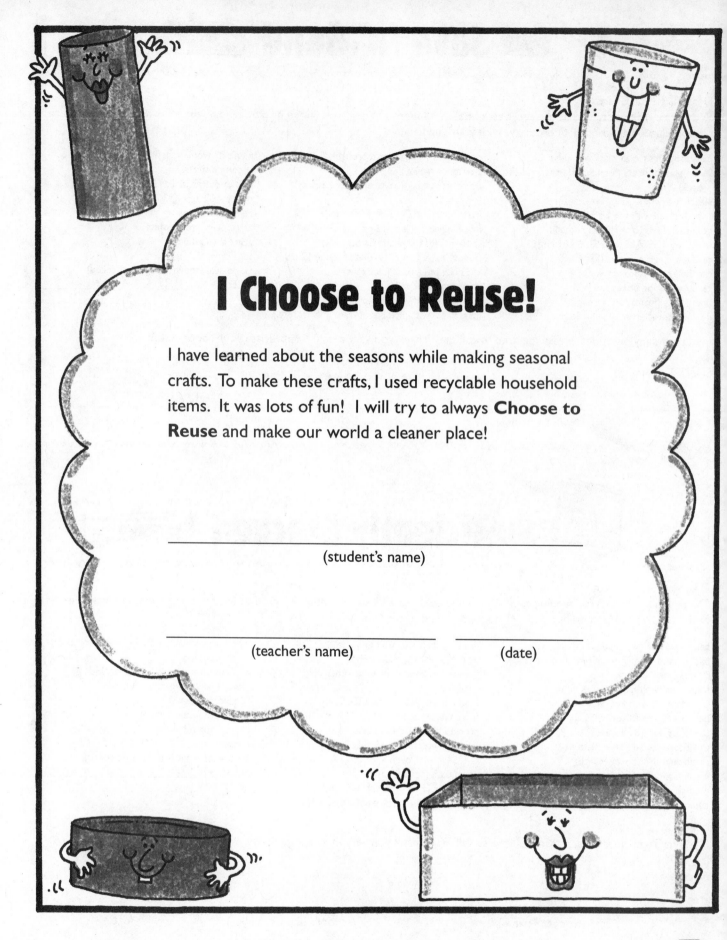

I Choose to Reuse!

I have learned about the seasons while making seasonal crafts. To make these crafts, I used recyclable household items. It was lots of fun! I will try to always **Choose to Reuse** and make our world a cleaner place!

_____

(student's name)

_____

(teacher's name)   (date)